NATURE WATCH
WOLVES

JEN GREEN

Consultant: Douglas Richardson
Zoological Director, Rome Zoo

C O N

Published by Anness Publishing Ltd,
Blaby Road, Wigston, Leicestershire LE18 4SE
Email: info@anness.com
Web: www.annesspublishing.com

Anness Publishing has a new picture agency outlet
for images for publishing, promotions or advertising.
Please visit our website www.practicalpictures.com
for more information.

Publisher: Joanna Lorenz
Managing Editor: Gilly Cameron Cooper
Senior Editor: Nicole Pearson
Designer: Ann Samuel
Picture Researcher: Cathy Stastny
Illustrators: Peter Bull, Vanessa Card, Sarah Smith
Production: Yolande Denny

ETHICAL TRADING POLICY
Because of our ongoing ecological investment
programme, you, as our customer, can have the
pleasure and reassurance of knowing that a tree is
being cultivated on your behalf to naturally replace
the materials used to make the book you are holding.
For further information about this scheme, go to
www.annesspublishing.com/trees

© Anness Publishing Ltd 2002, 2011

PUBLISHER'S NOTE
Although the advice and information in this book are
believed to be accurate and true at the time of going to
press, neither the authors nor the publisher can accept
any legal responsibility for any errors or
omissions that may have been made.

PICTURE CREDITS: b=bottom, t=top, c=centre,
l=left, r=right
Bryan and Cherry Alexander Photography: back cover
tr, 23tr, 26br, 27tl, 28t, 57br, 45c, 61cr; Ardea London:
John Daniels: 10b & 11tl; Chris Martin Bahr: 11cl;
Jean Paul Ferrero: 18b, 33t, 57c; Liz Bonford 26bl;
Stefan Meyers: 44b; Francois Gohier: 46t; M.
Krishnan: 47tl; The Art Archive: 55tl George Catlin;
BBC Natural History Unit: Francoise Savigny: back
cover cbl, 24tr, ; Simon King: back cover br, 36t, 37bl,
46br; C. Hamilton James: 2bl, 6b, 59br, Pete Oxford:
5t, 20bl, 47tr; Tom Vezo:4l, 19br, 63bl; Bernard
Castelein: 2-3c; Louis Gagnon: 5cr; Jeff Foott: 6tr; Pete
Oxford: 7cr; Tony Heald: 9c; R. Couper Johnston: 9b;
Keith Scholes: 15br; Richard Tu Tout: 19tr; Lockwood
and Dattatri: 25tl, 33br; Richard Du Toit: 25b;
Andrew Harrington: 29tl; Christopher Becker: 29tr;
Vadim Sidorovich: 30t; Lynn M. Stone: 45b;
Bernard Walton 51t; Ron O'Connor: 57br;
Lynn Stone: 61tr;The Bridgeman Art Library:
32t, 47br; Bruce Coleman Collection: Gunter
Ziesler: back papers, 24b; Hans Reinhard: 5b
& 5br; 15br; Rod Williams: 19tl, 41cl; Bruce
Davidson: 54t & b, 35cl; Erwin & Peggy
Bauer: 40t, 41b, 51bl; Staffan Widstrand:
42b; Rita Meyer: 46bl; Atlantide: 54b;
Jeff Foot: 57t; Mary Evans Picture
Library: 41cr, 54t, 55bl, 58bl, 58br;

Gettyone Stone Images: Roy Corral: cover cl; Tony Davis:
cover cr; back cover cr; Art Wolf: back cover cr, 27tr,
Rosemary Calvert: 21c; Kathy Bushue: 41tl; 42cr; The Kobal
Collection: 55tr; NHPA: Gerard Lacz: cover tl, 19c; Andy Rouse:
cover tr; back cover bl, 2tr; 26t, 59tl, Stephen Krasemann: cover
br, 60t, 61bl, 63br; Martin Harvey: 2t, 7tr; Jany Sauvanet 17c,
45cl, 53tr & b; T. Kitchin & V. Hurst:17br, 33br, 49c & b;
Rich Kirchner: 25c 36b; K. Ghani: 31t; Mirko Stelzner: 45t;
Oxford Scientific Films: Daniel J. Cox: cover, back cover tc,
back cover tr, : 2br , 15cr, 16tl, 16bl, 20tl, 25bl, 27b, 37cr, 38t,
49cl, 63t, 64t & b; Victoria McCormick: 1c, 20br, ; Nick Gordon
8t, 62bl;Charles Palek: 15tr; Stan Osolinski: 15tr; Steve Turner:
18t; Lon E. Lauber: 22t, 25cr, 35bl, 49tr, 62cr; Konrad Wothe:
22br, 57t; Alan and Sandy Carey: 25tl; Krupaker Senani: 29c;
Peter Weiman: 29b; Richard Day: 30b; Michael Leach: 51cl;
Anthony Bannister: 31cr; Michael Sewell: 51b; David Cayless:
35t,cr &b; M & C Tibbles: 58b; Matthews/Purdy: 39bl;
Richard Packwood: 40b; Colin Willcock: 45tl; Tom Ulrich:
43tr; Mike Hill: 44t; Vivek Sinha: 45cr; Villarosa/Overseas:
45b; Joe McDonald: 47bl; Bob Bennett: 48b; Rafi
Ben-Shahar: 56t, 61tl; Joel Bennett: 56b; Steve Turner:
57bl; Anna Walsh: 59bl; Claude Steelman: 59t; Owen
Newman: 59cr; Matthias Breiter: 60b; Papilio
Photographic: 48t; Peter Newark's Pictures:
15bl;Planet Earth Pictures: Ken Lucas: 15tl; Science
Photo Library: George Bernard: 51c, 62t; Still
Pictures: John Newby: back cover cbr, 52t;
Klein/Hubert: 7cl; 52bl & br; Warren
Photographic/Jane Burton: 21tl.

T E N T S

What is a Wolf?

Wolves are the wild members of the dog family, canids, with gleaming yellow eyes and lean, muscular bodies. The 37 different species of canids include wolves, jackals, coyotes, foxes and wild and domestic dogs. Canids are native to every continent except Australia and Antarctica. All of them share a keen sense of smell and hearing, and are carnivores (meat-eaters). Wolves and wild dogs hunt live prey, which they kill with their sharp teeth. However, many canids also eat vegetable matter and even insects. They are among the most intelligent of all animals. Some, such as wolves, are social in habit and live together in groups.

large, triangular ears, usually held pricked (erect)

powerful shoulders and supple body

▲ PRODUCING YOUNG
A female wolf suckles (feeds) her cubs. All canids are mammals and feed their young on milk. Females produce a litter of cubs, or pups, once a year. Most are born in an underground den.

BODY FEATURES ▶
The wolf is the largest wild dog. It has a strong, well-muscled body covered with dense, shaggy fur, a long, bushy tail and strong legs made for running. Its muzzle (nose and jaws) is long and well developed and its ears are pricked up. Male and female wolves look very similar, although females are generally the smaller of the two.

4

◄ KEEN SENSES

The jackal, like all dogs, has very keen senses. Its nose can detect faint scents and its large ears pick up the slightest sound. Smell and hearing are mainly used for hunting. Many canids also have good vision.

The Big, Bad Wolf

Fairy tales often depict wolves as wicked, dangerous animals. In the tale of the Three Little Pigs, the big, bad wolf terrorizes three small porkers. Eventually he is outwitted by the smartest pig, who builds a brick house that the wolf cannot blow down, and all the pigs are safe.

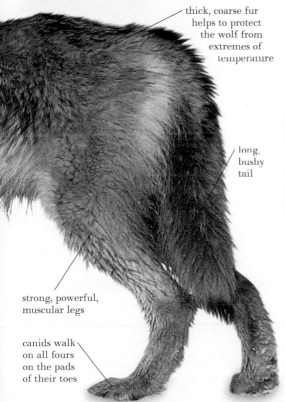

thick, coarse fur helps to protect the wolf from extremes of temperature

long, bushy tail

strong, powerful, muscular legs

canids walk on all fours on the pads of their toes

▲ LIVING IN PACKS

Wolves and a few other wild dogs live in groups called packs of about 8 to 20. Each pack has a hierarchy (social order) and is led by the strongest male and female.

EXPERT HUNTERS ►

A wolf bares its teeth in a snarl to defend its kill. Wolves and other canids feed mainly on meat, but eat plants, too, particularly when they are hungry.

The Wolf Family

Wolves were once common throughout the northern hemisphere, right across North America, Europe and Asia. In the past, people hunted them mercilessly. In many areas they died out altogether. Across the north, wolves from various regions may look quite different, but they are all one species, *Canis lupus*. However, there are many subspecies (different types). Two of the main types are the grey wolf, also known as the timber wolf, and the Arctic, or tundra wolf. Many other subspecies are named after the area or habitat they come from, such as Mexican and steppe wolves. The same type of wolf may be known by different names in different areas. For example, the Arctic wolf is the same as the tundra wolf. The wolf's closest relatives are the coyote, the jackal, the dingo and the domestic dog.

▲ **NEARLY EXTINCT**
The red wolf (*Canis rufus*) is found only in the south-eastern USA. It was once widespread, but became extinct in the wild. Today's red wolves stem from captive-bred wolves. They have longer legs and larger ears than the grey wolf and are named after the reddish fur on their heads, ears and legs. The grey wolf is thought to be a hybrid (cross) between the coyote and the wolf.

▼ **MOUNTAIN HOME**
The Simien wolf is found only in the Simien Mountains of Ethiopia, East Africa. It is about the same size as a coyote (1m long) and has a mainly reddish-brown coat, with pale fur on its belly and throat. The Simien wolf was once thought to be a kind of jackal. Now scientists have found out that it is a small wolf.

Did you know? Wolves kill prey animals as large as bison and as small as mice.

Simien wolf
(*Canis simensis*)

dingo
(Canis familiaris)

◄ DOG WITH NO BARK

The dingo lives in Australia and South-east Asia. It is now wild, but its ancestors are descended from tame dogs that Aboriginal people brought to the region from Asia more than 8,000 years ago. Dingoes are found mainly in dry areas such as the dusty Australian interior. They live in small families, and sometimes join other dingo families to hunt.

JACKAL ►

Jackals (*Canis lantrans*) are found on the grassy plains and in the woodlands of Africa, south-eastern Europe and southern Asia. They live in pairs and stay with the same mate for life. There are three species of jackal side-striped and black-backed jackals (found only in Africa) and golden jackals.

black-backed jackal
(Canis mesomelas)

▲ COYOTE

The coyote (*Canis latrans*) is found in North and Central America. It mainly lives on prairies (grassy plains) and in open woodlands and is also known as the prairie or brush wolf. Full-grown coyotes are half the size of grey wolves. They live alone, or in pairs and small family groups.

miniature poodle
(Canis familiaris)

◄ DOMESTIC DOG

You may not have seen a wolf in the wild, but you will know one of its relatives, for all domestic dogs are descended from the wolf. Dogs were the first animals to be tamed by people over 12,000 years ago. Now there are over 400 breeds of dog, including the miniature poodle.

bush dog
(Speothos venaticus)

Wild Dogs

In addition to the wolf's immediate family, five species of wild dog are distantly related to wolves and to each other. Foxes are also canids but are not closely related to wild dogs or wolves. Of the wild dogs, the bush dog and maned wolf are both found in South America. The dhole and raccoon dog come from eastern Asia. The African hunting dog lives in central and southern Africa. Like other canids, the bodies of these animals are adapted to suit their way of life and their environment. Raccoon dogs and bush dogs are short-legged species that make their homes in underground burrows. Maned wolves and African hunting dogs have long legs to help them see over the long grass and scrub of savannas (grasslands) and woodlands. Human settlements are currently expanding in the areas where these wild dogs live and threatening their existence.

▲ **STURDY HUNTER**
The bush dog inhabits forests and marshes in Central and South America. It is stocky, with a brown coat and paler fur on its neck and head.

◄ **FOXY CORGI**
The dhole (*Cuon alpinus*) can be found in India and China, on the islands of Sumatra and Java, and also in parts Russia. Adult dholes reach about 1m long, but have short legs. With their reddish coats, they look a little like corgis with long, bushy tails. Dholes live in packs and do much of their hunting during the day.

Classification Chart

Kingdom	*Animalia*	all animals
Phylum	*Chordata*	animals with backbones
Class	*Mammalia*	hair-covered animals that feed their young on milk
Order	*Carnivora*	mammals that eat meat
Family	*Canidae*	all dogs
Genus Species	*Cuon alpinus*	dhole

▲ CLASSIFICATION OF WILD DOGS

All wolves and wild dogs are canids (members of the dog family). Wolves and their close relatives belong to the genus (group) *Canis*, but the wild dogs shown here each belong to a different genus. The African hunting dog's scientific name (*Lycaon pictus*) is completely different from the dhole's (*Cuon alpinus*).

▲ MASKED HUNTER

The raccoon dog (*Nyctereutes procyonoides*) is found in eastern Europe, Siberia, China and Japan. Small in size, it reaches only 55cm long and has a chunky build. Its summer coat is grey-brown, with darker eye patches like a raccoon's mask. Its winter coat is white. These dogs live alone or in small groups.

HAPPY IN A CROWD ▶

The African hunting dog lives on the grassy plains south of the Sahara Desert. This wild dog has a mottled coat, long legs and rounded ears. It grows to about 1.1m long. African hunting dogs, like wolves, are social animals and live in packs. Males and females look very much alike and live to around the age of ten years old.

African hunting dog (*Lycaon pictus*)

◀ SHY LONER

The maned wolf (*Chrysocyon brachyurus*) lives in grasslands and swampy regions in eastern South America. Despite its name, this animal is not a wolf. Although its long legs have earned it the nickname 'the fox on stilts', it is not a fox either. Maned wolves have mostly reddish fur with darker legs and a mane of long hair at the neck. They grow to about 1.2m long. Solitary and shy, the wolves usually hunt at night.

Focus on

The skeletons of dogs buried with their owners in ancient tombs show that dogs have been domesticated for at least 12,000 years. All domestic dogs are descended from the wolf. The first dogs were probably bred from wolves tamed by hunters. These may have been captured as cubs and brought back to camp to help with hunting. Later, ancient peoples began to develop different breeds of dogs by selecting animals with definite features that they valued. From these beginnings developed the 400 different breeds we know today. Domestic dogs come in an amazing variety of shapes and sizes, from the tiny chihuahua to the huge St Bernard. Modern breeders divide the breeds into six main families: hounds, gundogs, working dogs, terriers, toys and utility (useful) dogs.

ANCIENT BREED
The pharaoh hound is one of the world's oldest dog breeds. It was developed in Egypt around 4,000 years ago as a swift hunting dog. Other breeds, such as the fierce mastiff, were developed as guard dogs. By Roman times, around 500BC, many of the breeds we know today had already been developed.

WORKING DOG
Border collies are working dogs and are used to herd sheep. The Border collie came from the Borders, an area on either side of the boundaries of England and Scotland. Working dogs have been bred to perform many useful tasks, from guarding homes to pulling sledges. This group includes corgis, boxers, mastiffs and huskies.

Domestic Dogs

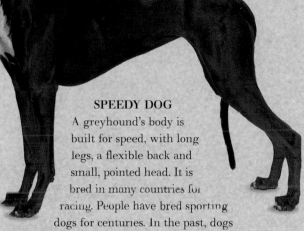

BRED TO FETCH AND CARRY

A golden retriever fetches a duck shot by its owner. Retrievers, setters, labradors and pointers are all gundogs, bred to help with hunting game birds. These naturally reliable and obedient dogs make good pets.

SPEEDY DOG

A greyhound's body is built for speed, with long legs, a flexible back and small, pointed head. It is bred in many countries for racing. People have bred sporting dogs for centuries. In the past, dogs were often bred for cruel sports such as bear-baiting. Today these sports are against the law in many countries.

HUNTING HOUNDS

A pack of foxhounds follow the scent of their quarry, a fox. Various breeds of hound have been developed to hunt different animals, including wolves, deer, rabbits, badgers and foxes. Foxhounds, beagles and bloodhounds track their prey by scent. Wolfhounds were bred to hunt wolves and deer. Afghan hounds were bred to chase antelope (similar to deer) and hunt by sight.

BURROWING EXPERT

The wire-haired fox terrier was very popular in England during the 1800s. The name terrier comes from the Latin *terra* (earth). All terriers were bred to hunt animals in burrows, such as foxes, rabbits, rats and badgers.

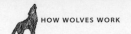
Body Shapes

Like all mammals, wolves and dogs are vertebrates (animals with backbones). The backbone protects the spinal cord, the main nerve of the body. The bones in the skeleton support the body and give it a distinct shape. The skeletons of wolves and dogs are different from other mammals. They have long skulls with large teeth, longish necks, and long, strong leg bones. Narrow collar bones help to make them slim and streamlined for speed over the ground, while their joints at the shoulders and hips pivot freely, giving them great agility. Wolves, foxes and wild dogs also generally have long tails. Many have a well-defined tail shape that can help to identify the animal at a distance.

backbone
(spine)

tail bones

toe bones

elastic ligaments and
tendons connect the
bones together

▲ TALL AND GRACEFUL

The maned wolf has longer leg bones than a true wolf. It uses them to hunt in the tall grass of its homeland. Its leg bones are weaker than a wolf's so it often lacks the power and strength to run down swift-moving prey. It has a short tail.

▲ BUILT FOR POUNCING

A fox's skeleton looks small and delicate compared to a wolf's. The leg bones are shorter in relation to its body size. Foxes spend much of their lives crouching and slinking through the undergrowth rather than running down prey.

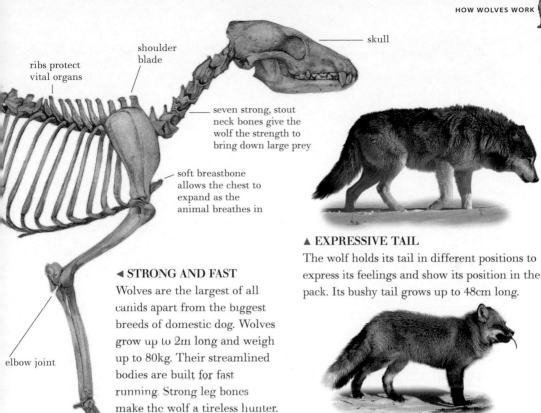

skull

shoulder blade

ribs protect vital organs

seven strong, stout neck bones give the wolf the strength to bring down large prey

soft breastbone allows the chest to expand as the animal breathes in

elbow joint

◄ STRONG AND FAST
Wolves are the largest of all canids apart from the biggest breeds of domestic dog. Wolves grow up to 2m long and weigh up to 80kg. Their streamlined bodies are built for fast running. Strong leg bones make the wolf a tireless hunter.

▲ EXPRESSIVE TAIL
The wolf holds its tail in different positions to express its feelings and show its position in the pack. Its bushy tail grows up to 48cm long.

▲ BALANCING BRUSH
The red fox's tail, known as a brush, is long and bushy. It grows up to 50cm long and helps to balance the animal when running and jumping.

▲ TAIL TALK
The African hunting dog's tail is short compared to most canids, about 30-40cm long. Its white tip stands out clearly and is used to signal other members of the pack.

Strong Like the Wolf
Native Americans admired the strength, courage and intelligence of wolves and wild dogs. Plains tribes such as the Blackfoot and Mandan formed warrior-bands called Dog Societies to honour the loyalty shown by wild dogs to other dogs in their pack. This Hidatsa shaman (medicine man) is dressed for the Dog Dance. Dances were performed in celebration and for good luck.

13

Body Parts

Muscular, fast-running wolves and wild dogs are built for chasing prey in open country. Thick muscles and long, strong legs enable them to run fast over great distances. The long skull helps the wolf to seize prey on the run. The wolf has a large stomach that can digest meat quickly and hold a big meal after a successful hunt. Wolves, however, can also go without food for more than a week if prey is scarce. Teeth are a wolf's main weapon, used for biting enemies, catching prey and tearing food. Small incisors (front teeth) strip flesh off bones. Long fangs (canines) grab and hold prey. Towards the back, jagged carnassial teeth close together like shears to chew meat into small pieces, while large molars can crush bones.

◀ POWERFUL MUSCLES
The muscles in the neck, shoulders and hindquarters of wolves and other canids are very well developed. These give the wolf strength and long-distance stamina as well as speed. Muscle-power alone is not enough, however, to catch prey. Wolves also need to use their cunning and stealth if the hunt is to succeed.

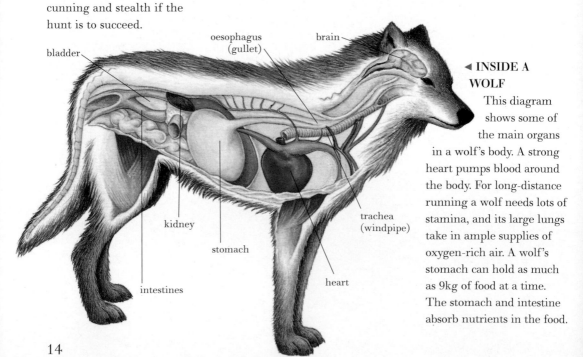

bladder

oesophagus (gullet)

brain

kidney

stomach

intestines

trachea (windpipe)

heart

◀ INSIDE A WOLF
This diagram shows some of the main organs in a wolf's body. A strong heart pumps blood around the body. For long-distance running a wolf needs lots of stamina, and its large lungs take in ample supplies of oxygen-rich air. A wolf's stomach can hold as much as 9kg of food at a time. The stomach and intestine absorb nutrients in the food.

14

▼ WOLF'S SKULL

A wolf's head has a broad crown and a tapering muzzle. The bones of the skull are strong and heavy. They form a tough case that protects the animal's brain, eyes, ears and nose. The jaws have powerful muscles that can exert great pressure as the wolf sinks its teeth in its prey.

molar   carnassial   canine   incisor

▼ BAT-EARED FOX SKULL

The bat-eared fox has a delicate, tapering muzzle. Its jaws are weaker than a wolf's and suited to deal with smaller prey, such as insects. This fox has 46–50 teeth, which is more than any other canid. Extra molars at the back of the animal's mouth enable it to crunch up insects, such as beetles, which have a tough outer casing on their bodies.

molar   carnassial   canine   incisor

▲ TIME FOR BED

A wolf shows its full set of meat-eating teeth as it yawns. Wolves and most other canids have 42 teeth. In wolves, the four large, dagger-like canines at the front of the mouth can grow up to 5cm long.

COOLING DOWN ▶

Like all mammals, the wolf is warm-blooded. This means its body temperature remains constant whatever the weather, so it is always ready to spring into action. Wolves do not have sweat glands all over their bodies as humans do, so in hot weather they cannot sweat to cool down. When the wolf gets too hot, it opens its mouth and pants with its large tongue lolling out. Moisture evaporates from the nose, mouth and tongue to cool the animal down.

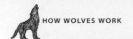

On the Move

Wolves are tireless runners. They can lope along for hours on end at a steady pace of 38km/h without resting. They have been known to cover an amazing 200km in a day searching for food. Compared to cheetahs, which can reach speeds of 96km/h over short distances, wolves are not fast runners. They can, however, put on a burst of speed to overtake fleeing prey.

Wolves and most other canids have four toes on their back feet and five toes on their front feet. The fifth toe on the front foot is called the dew claw, a small, functionless claw located a little way up on each front leg. They are more like pads than claws. They also have tough pads on the underside of their toes to help absorb the impact shock as the wolf's feet hit the ground.

▲ **SPEEDING COYOTE**
Like wolves, coyotes are good long-distance runners. They run on their toes, like all canids. This helps them to take long strides and so cover more ground. If necessary, coyotes can trot along for hours in search of food.

Did you know? Studies of wolves in the USA show one pack travelled 1,125km in 40 days.

◄ **IN MID-LEAP**
Strong leg muscles enable a wolf to leap long distances – up to 4.5m in a single bound. Wolves and other canids are very agile and can leap upwards, sideways and even backwards. As the wolf lands, its toes splay out to support its weight and prevent it from slipping.

grey wolf
(*Canis lupus*)

ankle joint

bones in the
foreleg are
fused together

toe bone

LONG TOE ▶
This close-up of the
bones in a maned wolf's
foreleg shows the long toe
bones that are used for
walking. The bones in the
foreleg, after the ankle joint
and before the toes, are fused together for
greater strength. Of all the canids, only the
African hunting dog does not have dew claws.

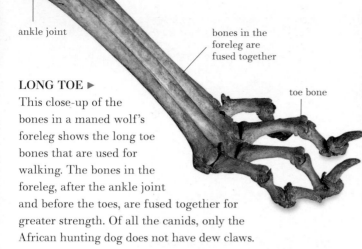

IN THE SWIM ▶
Bush dogs make their
homes near streams
and rivers and spend
much of their lives in
water. They are
strong swimmers, and
water creatures such
as capybaras (a type
of rodent) form part
of their diet. Wolves,
dingoes and most
other canids can also
swim well.

▲ WOLF TRACK
Clawmarks show up clearly in
a line of wolf prints in a snowy
landscape. Unlike cats, wolves
and wild dogs cannot retract
(draw in) their claws. When
walking, the wolf places its
paws almost in a straight line,
to form a single track. The
pawprints of a running wolf
are more widely spaced.

A KEEN CLIMBER ▶
Wolves and wild dogs are quick on the ground,
but they cannot climb trees. Some foxes,
however, climb well. The grey fox of North
America is an expert climber. It scrambles up
trees to steal birds' eggs and chicks. It also
climbs to get a good view over surrounding
countryside when searching for prey.

grey fox
(Urocyon cinereoargenteus)

17

Fur Coats

black-backed jackal
(Canis mesomelas)

Wolves and other members of the dog family have thick fur coats. This dense layer of hair helps to protect the animal's body from injury, and keeps it warm in cold weather. Wolves and other canids that live in cold places have extra-thick fur. Dingoes, jackals and wild dogs that live in warm countries close to the Equator have sparser fur. The fur is made up of two layers. Short dense underfur helps to keep the animal warm. Long guard hairs on top have natural oils that repel snow and rain to keep the underfur dry. A wild dog's fur coat is usually black, white or tan, or a mixture of these colours. Markings and patterns on the fur act as camouflage to disguise these animals, so they can creep up unseen on their prey.

▲ JACKAL COLOURS

The three species of jackal can be distinguished by their different markings. As its name suggests, the black-backed jackal has a dark patch on its back as well as brown flanks and a pale belly. The golden jackal is sandy-brown all over. The side-striped jackal is so named because of the light and dark stripes that run along its sides.

◄ WAITING FOR SPRING

Two raccoon dogs shelter under a bush waiting for the snow to melt. They already have their summer coats of grey with pale and dark patches. This will help to camouflage them among the summer grasses and vegetation. In autumn, they will moult (shed) these coats and grow a pure-white coat, ready for the winter snow.

◄ MANES AND RUFFS

The maned wolf gets its name from the ruff of long hairs on its neck. This may be dark or reddish-brown in colour. Wolves also have a ruff of longer hairs which they raise when threatened to make themselves look larger.

Arctic wolf
*(Canis lupus
tundarum)*

▲ HANDSOME CAMOUFLAGE

African hunting dogs have beautiful markings, with tan and dark-grey patches on their bodies, and paler, mottled fur on their heads and legs. The patterns work to break up the outline of their bodies as they hunt in the dappled light of the bush.

▲ WARM COAT

The Arctic wolf has very thick fur to keep it warm in icy temperatures. Its winter coat is pure white so that it blends in with the snow. In spring, the thick fur drops out and the wolf grows a thinner coat for summer. This coat is usually darker to match the earth without its covering of snow.

grey wolf
(Canis lupus)

VARYING COLOURS ►

Grey wolves vary greatly in colour, from pale silver to buff, sandy, red-brown or almost black. Even very dark wolves usually have some pale fur, often a white patch on the chest.

Sight and Sound

Wolves have excellent hearing. They can hear the sound of a snapping twig up to 3km away and are alert to the smallest noise that might give away the presence of potential prey. Wolves hear a wider range of sounds than humans. They can hear ultrasounds (very high-pitched noise) that are too high for human ears to catch. This means they can track down mice and other rodents in the dark. Sight is less important than hearing for hunting. Wolves are good at spotting movement, even at a great distance, but find it harder to see objects that keep still. Canids that hunt at night rely on sound and smell rather than sight. African hunting dogs and dholes, however, hunt by day, often in open country, and have keener sight.

▲ PRICKED EARS
Wolves cock (turn) their ears in different directions to pinpoint distant sounds. Even a tiny noise betrays the hiding place of a victim.

Coyote
(*Canis latrans*)

▲ LISTENING IN
An African hunting dog's large, rounded ears work like satellite dishes to gather sound. Keen hearing is vital in the hunt and allows pack members to keep in touch amongst the undergrowth.

HOWLING HELLO ▶
Coyotes and other wild dogs keep in touch with distant members of their group by howling. The coyote call is actually a series of yelps that ends in a long wail.

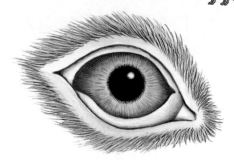

Did you know? African hunting dogs chatter like monkeys as they play together.

◄ BARKING MAD

Some domestic dogs, such as this German shepherd, have been bred to bark loudly to warn their owners of approaching strangers. Wolves also bark if they meet an intruder near the den, but more quietly and less aggressively.

▲ A THIRD EYELID

Wolves' eyes have a third eyelid, called a nictating (blinking) membrane. This membrane is inside their upper and lower eyelids, and sweeps over the surface of the eye when the wolf blinks. It protects the eyes from dust and dirt that might damage it otherwise.

◄ GLOWING EYES

Wolves have round, yellow eyes. In dark conditions, a layer at the back of the eye, called the *tapetum lucidum*, intensifies what little light there is. This allows a wolf to see at night. The layer also reflects light, making the wolf's eyes glow in the dark if a strong light is shone into them.

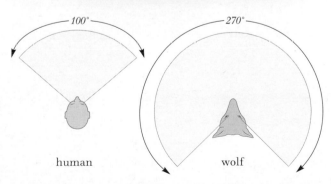

— 100° —   — 270° —

human   wolf

◄ WOLF VISION

Wide-set eyes in the front of its face give a wolf a very wide field of vision. As the view from each eye overlaps, binocular vision (using both eyes at the same time) allows a wolf to focus at close range and pounce on its prey.

21

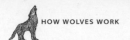

Smell, Touch and Taste

Of all the senses, smell is the most important for wolves and wild dogs. These animals are constantly surrounded by different scents and their keen sense of smell can distinguish them all. They follow the scent trails left behind by other animals in their quest for food, and can pick up even faint whiffs of scent on the wind. This helps them to work out the direction of distant prey. Canids that hunt in packs use scent to identify and communicate with other pack members. They also communicate by sight and touch.

Like other mammals, wolves and wild dogs have taste buds on their tongues to taste their food. They eat foods they find the tastiest first. The tongue is also used to lap up water.

▲ **TRACKING PREY**
Nose to the ground, a wolf follows a scent trail in the snow. From the scent a wolf can tell what type of animal left it, whether it is well or ill, how far away it is and whether another wolf is following the trail.

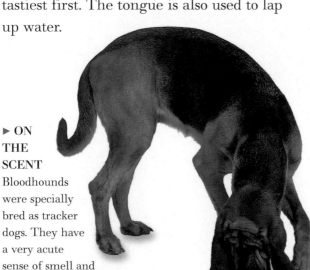

► **ON THE SCENT**
Bloodhounds were specially bred as tracker dogs. They have a very acute sense of smell and can follow a scent that is several days old. They keep their noses very close to the ground. Their drooping ears help to channel scent into the nose.

▲ **PLEASED TO MEET YOU**
When two wolves meet they sniff the glands at the base of the tail. Pack members all have a familiar scent. Scent is also used to signal mood, such as contentment or fear, or if a female is ready to breed.

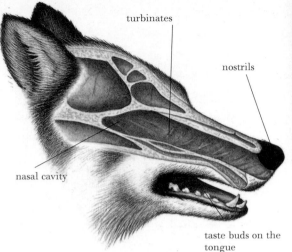

▲ **INSIDE THE SNOUT**

Inside a wolf's snout is a large nasal cavity used for smelling. Scent particles pass over tubes of very thin bone in the roof of the nasal cavity. These tubes, called turbinates, are connected to a nerve network that sends signals to the brain.

▲ **TOUCHY-FEELY**

Wolves use touch to bond with each other. They rub bodies, lick one another and thrust their noses into each other's fur when they meet. Pack members play-fight by wrestling with locked jaws, or chasing around in circles.

▼ **SENSITIVE NOSE**

The wolf's leathery outer nose is set right at the end of its snout. Two nostrils draw air laden with scents into the nasal cavity. The wolf may flare its nostrils to take in extra air. The animal may lick its nose before scenting, because a damp nose helps its sense of smell. Long, sensitive whiskers on either side of the snout are used for touching things at close range.

▲ **WELL GROOMED**

A wolf nibbles at the tufts of hair between its paw pads. It is removing ice that might cut and damage the paw. Wolves groom (clean) their fur to keep it in good condition. Licking and running fur through the teeth helps to remove dirt and dislodge fleas.

Living Together

Wolves are very social animals. A few may live alone, but most live in packs. A wolf pack may contain as few as 2 or as many as 36 animals. Most packs have between 8 and 24 members. The main purpose of the pack is to hunt. A team of wolves working together can hunt down and kill much larger and stronger prey than a wolf would be able to on its own. Only the strongest, healthiest pair in the wolf pack will actually mate. Every pack member then helps to feed and bring up the cubs. Bush dogs, dholes and African hunting dogs also live in packs, while jackals, and sometimes coyotes and raccoon dogs, live in smaller family groups. Maned wolves and foxes usually live alone.

▲ TWO'S COMPANY
A pair of jackals drinks from a waterhole in South Africa. Some jackals are solitary, but most pair up for life. The cubs are reared in small, close-knit family groups. Older brothers or sisters often help their parents to rear the small cubs.

Did you know? Foxes produce alarming screams when looking for a mate.

WOLF PACK ▶
A wolf pack is led by the strongest, most experienced animals. The rest of the pack often consists of their children – young cubs and older, half-grown wolves. The young wolves follow their leaders until they are old enough to leave the pack.

maned wolf
(*Chrysocyon brachyurus*)

▲ A FAMILY AFFAIR

Dholes live in family packs of between 5 and 12 animals. Sometimes several families join together to form a very large dhole pack called a clan. Hunting in a big group helps these relatively small wild dogs to tackle large prey such as wild cattle and buffalo.

▲ EACH FOR ITSELF

The maned wolf is mostly solitary, living and hunting on its own. Males and females pair up during the breeding season. The male helps to feed and rear his pups – as do all canids, except for the domestic dog.

◄ COYOTE COUPLE

Most coyotes live and hunt alone, in pairs or in small family units. Sometimes, several of these small groups band together to make a bigger hunting party to go after large prey.

DOG SOCIETY ►

African hunting dogs are the next most social canids after wolves. They hunt co-operatively and all pack members help to raise the pups of the breeding pair. The males in the pack are all brothers. Females often join from a different pack.

Focus on

A wolf pack has a strict social order and each member knows its place. The senior male and female, known as the alpha male and female, are the only animals to breed. The alpha male takes the lead in hunting, defends the pack members from enemies, and keeps the other animals in their place. In most packs, a second pair of wolves, called the beta male and female, come next in the ranking order. The other pack members are usually the offspring of the alpha pair, aged up to three years old.

LEADER OF THE PACK
An alpha male wolf greets a junior pack member. Wolves use different body positions and facial expressions to show rank. The leader stands upright with tail held high. The junior has his ears laid back and his tail tucked between his legs.

IT'S A PUSHOVER
A junior wolf rolls over on its back in a gesture of submission to a more dominant pack member. A junior wolf can also pacify a stronger animal by imitating cub behaviour, such as begging for food.

SHOWING WHO IS BOSS
A wolf crouches down to an alpha male. The young wolf whines as it cowers, as if to say, 'You're the boss'. The pack leader's confident stance makes him look as large as possible.

a Wolf Pack

'I GIVE IN'

A male grey wolf lays its ears back and sticks its tongue out. Taken together, these two gestures signal submission. A wolf with its tongue out, but its ears pricked, is sending a different message, showing it feels hostile and rebellious.

REJECTED BY THE PACK

Old, wounded or sickly wolves are often turned out of the pack to become lone wolves. Although pack members may be affectionate with each other, there is no room for sentiment. Young wolves may also leave to start their own packs. Lone wolves without the protection of a pack are much more vulnerable to attack and must be more cautious.

SCARY SNARL

A grey wolf bares its canine teeth in a snarl of aggression. Studies have shown that wolves use up to 20 different facial expressions. Junior wolves use snarling expressions to challenge the authority of their leaders. The alpha male may respond with an even more ferocious snarl. If it does so, the junior wolf is faced with a choice. It must back down, or risk being punished with a nip.

Home Territory

Territories are areas that animals use for finding food or for breeding. An animal will defend its territory against others that might provide competition. Wolf packs use their territories as hunting grounds and also as safe places to raise their cubs. Wolf territories vary in size, depending on how much food is available to feed the pack. Small territories cover about 100 sq km. Large territories may be 10 or even 100 times this size. At the heart of the territory is the rendezvous, a meeting place where the wolves gather. This place also acts as a nursery where older cubs are left to play. The borders of the territory are patrolled by the pack on a regular basis, and marked with urine. Strong-smelling urine sprayed at marker sites lasts several days, while howling also serves as a long-distance warning. The pack will defend its territory fiercely if a rival pack tries to enter.

▲ KEEP TO THE TRAIL

A pack of wolves runs along a snowy trail in single file. Each wolf treads in the tracks of the one in front. This saves a lot of energy that would be wasted if each animal broke a separate trail through the deep snow. Wolves use well-worn paths inside their territories. These connect meeting places with lookout points and good ambush sites.

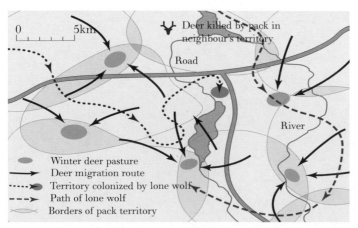

◄ NEIGHBOURING TERRITORIES

Several wolf territories may lie close to each other. Where food is plentiful, for example where deer breed, territories may overlap (see diagram). Rivers, towns and roads form natural boundaries. There may be a neutral 1km wide no-go area between territories. If food becomes scarce, however, wolves will enter this zone.

▲ SCENT SIGNAL

A wolf smells a rock that another pack member has marked with urine. The scent lingers for several days after the animal has moved on. A wolf smelling this signal can tell how many animals have passed this way and whether they belong to its pack. Wolves from a rival pack will mark the other side of the rock to reinforce territory boundaries.

▲ BORDER DISPUTE

A wolf snarls at a wolf from another pack on the boundary between their territories. When food is scarce, packs are more likely to trespass or raid each other's territory. In times of plenty, scent signals keep trespassers out, so border disputes are rare.

◄ SCENT-MARKING

A dhole marks the edge of its territory by spraying urine on a patch of grass. Some canids, such as African hunting dogs and foxes, leave piles of droppings too. In a wolf pack, it is usually the alpha male that marks the boundaries.

KEEP-OUT CALL ►

Three wolves raise their heads in a group howl. Each animal howls a slightly different note, making an eerie harmony. The sound carries over a long distance – 10km or more. If it reaches a rival pack, the other wolves may howl back. Howling is also used to rally the pack, for example, before a hunt.

A Meaty Diet

Wolves and their relatives are carnivores (meat-eaters). They kill prey for fresh meat, but also eat carrion (dead animals). When no meat is available wolves eat plants, such as fruit and berries, and also grass to aid digestion. Large herd animals such as musk oxen, moose, deer and caribou are the favourite targets of the wolf pack. All canids target other kinds of prey if a particular creature becomes scarce. For example, they hunt a wide range of smaller animals, including birds, hares, mice and beavers.

Wolves swim well and chase fish, frogs and crabs, but still spend much of their lives with empty bellies. When food is scarce, they sometimes approach towns and villages, where they rifle through rubbish or kill domestic sheep, goats, cattle and horses.

▲ NOT-SO-FUSSY FEEDERS
Raccoon dogs of eastern Asia are omnivores — they eat all kinds of different foods, including rodents, fruit and acorns. They are strong swimmers and catch frogs, fish and water beetles in streams and rivers. They also scavenge carrion and scraps from people's rubbish tips.

▼ COYOTE PREY
Three coyotes tear at the carcass of a moose. Coyotes usually hunt small prey such as mice, but sometimes they band together to go after larger creatures such as moose. Teams of coyotes also gang up on other predators and steal their kills.

◄ FAST FOOD

A pack of dholes makes quick work of a deer carcass. Each one eats fast to get its share. A hungry dhole can eat up to 4kg of meat in an hour. Mammals form a large part of a dhole's diet, but if meat is scarce a dhole will also eat berries, lizards and insects.

▲ MEAT AND FRUIT-EATER

A maned wolf lopes off in search of prey. Without a pack to help it hunt, it looks for easy prey, including armadillos and small rodents such as agoutis and pacas. It also feeds on birds, reptiles, frogs and insects, fruit and sugar cane.

▲ BEACH SQUABBLE

Two black-backed jackals squabble over the carcass of a seal pup. Jackals eat almost anything – fruit, frogs, reptiles and a wide range of mammals, from gazelles to mice. Jackals also scavenge kills from other hunters.

CACHING FOOD ►

A wolf looks for a suitable spot in the snow to bury a freshly caught hare. After a pack has killed a large beast, or when a lone hunter has eaten its fill, it hides the remains of its food. Then, when food is scarce, the wolf can return to the hidden cache and retrieve its kill.

grey wolf
(Canis lupus)

Did you know? All canids are quick feeders, but dholes in particular bolt their food down at a great rate.

Going Hunting

Wolves and wild dogs do not all hunt at the same time of day. Maned wolves, bush dogs and raccoon dogs are mainly nocturnal (active at night). They rely on smell and hearing to find their prey. Dholes and African hunting dogs are daytime hunters, and track their prey by sight as well as smell and sound. Wolves hunt at any time of day or night. Members of a wolf pack work together like players in a sports team. Each animal has particular strengths that help the group. Some wolves are good trackers, others are particularly cunning, fast, or powerful, and so help to bring down large animals such as moose. Wolves spend a lot of time searching for food. A hunt may last for several hours, but nine out of ten hunts are unsuccessful and the wolves go hungry. If they strike lucky, they might kill a beast large enough to provide meat for all the pack.

Little Red Riding Hood
In the story of Little Red Riding Hood, a cunning wolf eats Red Riding Hood's grandmother. The wolf then steals the old woman's clothes to prey on the little girl. Fortunately a wood cutter rescues Red Riding Hood in the nick of time. As he kills the wolf, the grandmother emerges alive from inside the wolf.

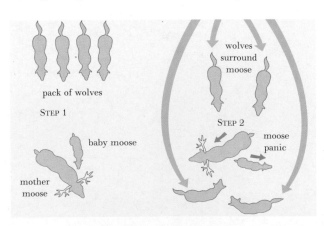

pack of wolves

STEP 1

mother moose

baby moose

wolves surround moose

STEP 2

moose panic

◄ **WOLF PACK IN ACTION**
Wolves use skill as well as strength to hunt large creatures such as moose. A moose calf is an easier target than a full-grown animal. The wolves stalk their prey, fanning out and running ahead to surround the victim. Pack members dash forward to panic the animals and separate the mother from her baby. Once the young calf is separated, the wolves run it down and kill it with a bite to the neck.

DINGO KILL ▶

Two dingoes have just caught a kangaroo. In the Australian outback, dingoes hunt a wide range of creatures, from tiny grasshoppers and lizards to large prey such as wild pigs and kangaroos. Sheep, introduced by settlers in the 1800s, are a favourite target.

◀ GROUP KILL

A large pack of wolves has killed a white-tailed deer. This amount of meat will not satisfy the group for long. Where food is scarce, territories are often much larger than in places where the hunting is easy. The pack will always hunt the largest game it can find.

Coyote
(Canis latrans)

CLEVER TACTICS ▶

A coyote plays with a mouse it has surprised in the snow. Coyotes often hunt mice, leaping high in the air to pounce on their victims. Coyotes have a more varied diet than wolves, feeding on fruit, grass, berries and insects, as well as mammals such as rabbits, deer and rodents. They take to water to catch fish and frogs, and also steal sheep and chickens, which makes them unpopular with farmers.

Did you know For peak condition, a wolf needs to eat 4kg of meat a day.

▲ TEAMWORK

Working as a team, dholes hunt large prey such as sambar (a type of deer). Dholes whistle to keep in touch with one another as they surround their prey. Teamwork also helps the pack to defend the kill from scavengers such as vultures.

Focus on African

African hunting dogs eat more meat than any other canid. One in every three of their hunts ends in a kill, a very high success rate. They live on the savanna (grassy plains) of central and southern Africa, which is also home to vast herds of grazing animals such as zebra, wildebeest and gazelle. The pack wanders freely over a huge area of savanna, looking for herd animals to prey on. They rely on sight to find their quarry, so they hunt during daylight hours or on bright moonlit nights. They mainly hunt at dusk or dawn when the air is coolest and rest in the shade during the hottest time of day.

1 A pack of wild dogs begins to run down their quarry, a powerful wildebeest. On the open plains of the Serengeti in East Africa, there is little cover that would allow the dogs to sneak up on their prey. The hunt is often therefore a straightforward chase. A junior dog may lead the hunt at first. The pack also targets many kinds of antelope, such as kudu and gazelle.

2 The dogs run along at an easy lope at first. They have tested out the wildebeest herd to find an easy target. They look for weak, injured, or young and inexperienced animals that will make suitable victims. This wildebeest is an older animal whose strength may be failing.

Hunting Dogs

3 A hunting dog tries to seize the wildebeest's tail. Hunting dogs with different strengths and skills take on different roles during the hunt. The lead dogs are super-fit and strong. They dodge out of the way if the wildebeest turns to defend itself with its sharp hooves and horns. Fast runners spread out to surround the victim and cut off its escape.

4 As the wildebeest tires, two dogs grip its snout and tail, pinning it down. Hunting dogs can run at 50km/h for quite a distance, but their prey is much swifter. While the lead dogs follow the fleeing animal's twists and turns, backmarkers take a more direct line, saving their strength. The rear dogs take over the chase as the leaders tire.

5 More dogs arrive and the strongest move in for the kill. While some dogs hold their victim by the snout and flanks, others jump up to knock it off balance. The dogs attack their victim's sides and rump and soon the animal is bleeding freely. It begins to weaken through shock and loss of blood.

6 The wildebeest crashes to the ground and the dogs rip at its underparts to kill it. There is little snapping and snarling as they eat, but the kill is fiercely defended if a scavenger such as a jackal comes close. Half-grown cubs feed first, then the carcass is ripped apart and bones, skin and all are eaten. Back at the den young cubs are fed with pre-chewed meat.

Finding a Mate

Wolves and wild dogs breed once a year, towards the end of winter. The cubs are born roughly two months later, in the spring. The size of the litter varies from species to species. Maned wolves give birth to the fewest young, usually only two cubs. Each pregnant wolf produces between three and eight cubs per litter. African hunting dogs have the largest litters: up to 16 pups at a time.

About six weeks after mating, a female wolf prepares a den in a cave, a hollow tree trunk or an underground burrow. Here her cubs will be born. The pack gathers outside the den as she begins to give birth. They howl as if to encourage the mother as the young are born.

▲ PURE PEDIGREE

In some parts of Australia, dingoes live in packs, in which only the dominant female breeds. In other areas, they live in smaller family groups. Because there are no other wild dogs to breed with, dingoes are in fact the most pure bred dogs in the world. They are directly descended from prehistoric domestic dogs.

Did you know? Wolf cubs take about 63 days to develop in their mother's womb before they are born.

COURTING COUPLE ▶

A male wolf sniffs his partner to find out if she is ready to mate. Tensions run high in the wolf pack during the breeding season, as all the adult wolves are ready to breed. The alpha male and female must dominate the rest to make sure they are the only ones to mate. The alpha female temporarily drives the other females from the pack. Once the alpha pair have mated, all the wolves can relax.

◄ MATING WOLVES

When they mate, the male wolf mounts the female and grasps her sides with his front paws. The female becomes ready to mate as the periods of daylight grow longer. This means that her pups will be born in spring as the weather warms up and food becomes plentiful. In North America, in the south of their range, if mating is in February the cubs will be born in late April or May. Farther north, wolves give birth in May or June.

LOCKED TOGETHER ►

Directly after mating, canids often stay tied (locked together) for many minutes. Tying helps to ensure that the alpha male is the father of the cubs, rather than an alpha male from a rival pack that may mate with the alpha female afterwards. It also helps strengthen the bond between parent wolves.

◄ DINGO DEN

A rocky cave overlooking a stony desert makes a good den site for this mother dingo. The cave will be a safe, cool and shady place for the cubs to be born.

▲ GIVING BIRTH

A mother wolf licks her newborn cub to clean it and stimulate it to begin breathing. Wolf cubs are born at intervals of about 15 to 30 minutes, and it may take up to six hours for a large litter to be born.

Newborn Cubs

At birth the young of wolves and dogs are tiny and helpless. Newborn wolves are only about 21cm long from the tip of their short noses to the end of their thin, little tails. With eyes tightly closed, they cannot see or hear, or even stand on their weak legs. They squirm around and huddle close to their mother for warmth. Like all mammals, their first food is their mother's rich milk, which she encourages them to suck from the moment they are born.

After one or two weeks, the cubs' eyes open and they take notice of their surroundings. They take their first wobbly steps and scramble over each other in the den. At about five weeks, the cubs begin to take solid food as well as milk. Half-chewed meat, stored in the stomach of an adult wolf, is brought to the den and coughed up when the cubs beg for food.

▲ AT THE DEN
Wolf cubs take a first look at the big world outside their den. For nearly eight weeks their only experience has been the burrow – a 4m long tunnel dug in soft earth with room for an adult wolf to creep along. The cubs sleep in a cosy chamber at the end, while their mother sleeps in a hollow nearer the entrance.

Did you know? Young wolf cubs need to feed every few hours and drink 300ml of milk a day.

NURSING MOTHER ▶
The mother wolf hardly leaves her cubs for the first weeks of their lives. Her mate, and the other members of the pack, bring food so she does not need to leave the den to go hunting. As a nursing mother, she is always hungry and needs large quantities of food to produce enough milk to feed her hungry cubs.

▼ CUBS IN DANGER

These wolf cubs are about six or seven weeks old. Not all cubs are born in a den. Some are born in a hollow sheltered from the wind, or in a nest flattened in long grass. There are many dangers for cubs in the open. They may be snatched by predators such as bears or eagles. Many do not survive to adulthood.

grey wolf cubs
(Canis lupus)

Romulus and Remus

According to ancient Roman legend, Romulus and Remus were twin brothers who were abandoned as babies on a remote hillside. A she-wolf found them and brought them up, feeding them on her milk. Both brothers survived and Romulus went on to found the city of Rome.

▲ HUNGRY PUPPIES

An African hunting dog suckles her pups. They suck milk from two sets of nipples on her underside. Female hunting dogs often have more nipples than other canids, because they have the biggest litters and therefore the most mouths to feed. As the pups' sharp teeth begin to hurt she will wean them on to meat.

▲ RARE CUBS

In the mountains of Ethiopia, a Simien wolf guards her litter of five cubs. Simien wolves have similar breeding habits to other wolves, but are much rarer. These cubs look healthy, so have a good chance of surviving long enough to breed as adults.

39

Growing Up

At eight weeks old, wolf cubs are very lively. Their snouts have grown longer, their ears stand up and they look much more like adult wolves. They bound about on long, strong legs. Now weaned off milk, they live on a diet of meat brought by the adults. As they leave the safety of the den, the other pack members gather round and take great interest in the cubs. The cubs' new playground is the rendezvous, the safe place at the heart of wolf-pack territory where the adults gather. This is usually a sheltered, grassy spot near a stream where the cubs can drink. Here they develop their hunting skills by pouncing on mice and insects. In play-fights they establish a ranking order that mirrors the social order in the pack.

▲ CARRIED AWAY

A wolf carries a cub to safety by seizing the loose skin at the scruff of its neck in its teeth. This adult is most likely the cub's mother or father, but it may be another member of the pack. All the adult wolves are very tolerant with the youngsters to begin with. Later, as the cubs grow up, they may be punished with a well-placed nip if they are naughty.

Did you know? Father wolves make squeaking noises to call their cubs.

SHARING A MEAL ▶

A young African hunting dog begs for food by whining, wagging its tail and licking the adult's mouth. The adult responds by arching its back and regurgitating (bringing up) a meal of half-digested meat from its stomach. The pups grow quickly on this diet. At the age of four months, they are strong enough to keep up with the pack when they go hunting.

▼ PRACTICE MAKES PERFECT

Two Arctic fox cubs practise their hunting skills by pouncing on one another. Wolf cubs play-fight to establish a ranking order. By the age of 12 weeks, one cub has managed to dominate the others. He or she may go on to become leader of a new pack.

Wolfchild

Rudyard Kipling's Jungle Book, which was published in 1894, is set in India. The book tells the story of Mowgli, a young boy who is abandoned and brought up by wolves in the jungle. When Mowgli becomes a man he fights his arch-enemy, the tiger Shere Khan. Kipling's tale was inspired by many true-life accounts of wolf-children who grew up in the wild in India during the 1800s.

▲ YOUTHFUL CURIOSITY

Young maned wolves investigate their surroundings. Females usually bear three cubs at most. Newborn young have grey-brown fur, short legs and snouts. Later they develop long legs and handsome red fur.

ALMOST GROWN ▶

These two young wolves are almost full-grown. Cubs can feed themselves at about ten months, but remain with the pack to learn hunting skills. At about two or three years old, many are turned out. They wander alone or with brothers or sisters until they find a mate and start a new pack.

Icy Wastes

Wolves were once widespread throughout the northern hemisphere. As human settlements have expanded, so wolves have been confined to more remote areas such as the far north. The Arctic is a frozen wilderness where very few people live. Wolves and Arctic foxes are found here. On the barren, treeless plains known as the tundra, harsh, freezing winter weather lasts for nine months of the year. Both land and sea are buried beneath a thick layer of snow and ice. Few animals are active in winter, so prey is scarce. During the brief summer, the ice and snow melt, flowers bloom and birds, insects and animals flourish, so prey is abundant. Arctic wolves and foxes rear their cubs in this time of plenty. Another harsh, remote habitat, the windswept grass steppes of Asia, is home to the small steppe wolf.

Arctic Legend
Native Americans named natural phenomena after the animals that lived around them. The Blackfoot called the Milky Way the Wolf Trail. In northern Canada, the Cree believed the Northern Lights, shown below, shone when heavenly wolves visited the Earth. In fact these spectacular light shows in the Arctic are caused by particles from the Sun striking the Earth's atmosphere.

◄ **WHITE WOLF**
Arctic wolves are larger than most other wolf species. They scrape under the snow to nibble plant buds and lichen if they are desperate for food.

Did you know?
The largest Arctic wolf territories cover 13,000 km – an area about the same size as Northern Ireland.

Arctic wolf
(Canis lupus tundarum)

▲ WARM FUR

This Inuit girl is wearing a hood trimmed with wolf fur. The fur is warm and sheds the ice that forms on the hood's edge as the wearer breathes. The Inuit and other peoples of the far north traditionally dressed in the skins of Arctic animals. Animal skins make the warmest clothing and help to camouflage the wearer when hunting.

▲ ARCTIC HUNTER

A grey wolf feeds hungrily on a caribou carcass. In the icy north, wolves need very large territories to find enough prey. They will follow deer for hundreds of kilometres as the herds move south for the winter.

◀ ARCTIC HELPER

One crack of a whip brings a team of huskies under control. Tough and hardy huskies, with their thick fur coats, are the working dogs of the far north. They are used by the Inuit and other Arctic peoples to pull sledges and help to hunt.

SNOWY BED ▶

A grey wolf shelters in a snowy hollow to escape a howling blizzard. With its thick fur, it can sleep out in the open in temperatures as low as -46°C. Snow drifting over its body forms a protective blanket.

In the Forest

▲ WOODLAND JACKAL
A side-striped jackal keeps a wary look-out for danger. In Africa, the three different kinds of jackal are found in different types of terrain. Side-striped jackals keep mostly to woods and swampy areas. Golden and black-backed jackals live in more open countryside.

South of the treeless Arctic tundra, a belt of dense evergreen forests rings the northern hemisphere. It covers large parts of Canada, northern Europe and Russia. South of this belt lie the broad-leaved woodlands of temperate (warm) regions. Yet farther south, tropical rainforests grow in the hotter regions around the Equator.

Wolves and other canids flourish in forests and woods where there is a plentiful supply of prey and dense undergrowth in which to hide and stalk. Wolves are perhaps most at home in temperate northern regions, where large game such as deer abound. In tropical rainforests, most creatures live high in the tree-tops, where wild dogs cannot reach them. However, canids such as bush dogs and raccoon dogs are found near streams and rivers, which also teem with life.

◄ HIDDEN HUNTERS
In dark pine forests and dappled broad-leaved woodlands, the grey or blackish coats of wolves blend in with the shadows. This helps them to creep up on deer, moose, and other forest prey. Dense foliage also protects the wolves from the worst of the north's drenching rain.

Raccoon dog
(*Nyctereutes procyonoides*)

◄ SOUND SLEEPERS

Raccoon dogs live in thickly wooded river valleys in eastern Asia. They are the only canids that hibernate in winter. In autumn raccoon dogs gorge themselves on fruit and meat to put on a thick layer of fat. Then they retreat to their burrows. They sleep right through the harsh winter and wake in spring.

JUNGLE PACK ►

A dhole moves through the thick undergrowth of a forest in India. Packs of dholes hunt deer such as chital and sambar. They call to one another to surround their prey as it moves through the dense jungle. The pack will guard its kills against bears, tigers and scavengers.

◄ RODENTS BEWARE

Bush dogs live in the dense forests and marshlands of South America. In the wetlands, their main prey are aquatic rodents such as pacas and agoutis. These fierce dogs will even plunge into the water to hunt capybaras — the world's largest rodents, 1.3m long.

Did you know? Raccoon dogs are the only canids that cannot bark.

A SCARCE BREED ►

A wolf surveys the snowy landscape in the Abruzzo region of central Italy. Wolves are common in remote forests in Canada and Russia, but in western Europe they are scarce. They survive in small pockets of wilderness, hiding in the hills by day and creeping down to villages to steal scraps at night.

Grassland and Desert

Grasslands are found on every continent except Antarctica. Savanna (grassland) is home to several canids, including maned wolves, black-backed jackals and African hunting dogs. Other canids, including coyotes, dingoes and several kinds of fox, live in deserts. In these harsh, barren places, the sun beats down mercilessly by day, but at night the temperature plummets. Scorching daytime temperatures may cause animals to overheat. Desert foxes keep cool during the hot days by hiding under shady rocks or in dark burrows, emerging to hunt only at night. Another big problem for desert animals is lack of water. Wild dogs and foxes can survive for long periods with little water, or derive most of the liquid they need from their food.

▲ **DESERT WOLVES**
Wolves are found in deserts and dry areas in Mexico, Iran and Arabia. With little vegetation to provide cover, they stalk prey by hiding behind boulders or rocky outcrops. Desert wolves often have pale or sandy fur, to blend in with their surroundings.

▲ **GIVING OFF HEAT**
A black-backed jackal's large ears contain a network of fine veins. Blood flowing through these veins gives off heat, keeping the animal cool.

◄ **HUNTERS OF THE OUTBACK**
A pair of dingoes waits at a rabbit warren in central Australia. Dingoes have lived wild in the outback for more than 8,000 years. Their reddish-brown coats, with paler fur on their legs and bellies, are perfect camouflage in the desert landscape.

▲ OUTCAST DOGS

Feral dogs are the descendants of domestic dogs that have become wild. In Asia they are known as pariah (outcast) dogs. Feral dogs are very adaptable and change their behaviour to suit any situation. In India, pariah dogs hang around villages and sneak in to scavenge scraps.

▲ SMALLER PACKS

A pack of African hunting dogs tears a carcass apart. In the past, hunting dogs were numerous and widespread throughout central and southern Africa. Packs were large, containing 100 animals or more. Now these wild dogs are much more scarce and their packs are also smaller, usually containing between 6 and 30 animals.

▲ SLY HUNTER

A maned wolf hunts in the long grass in Argentinian marsh-land. Despite its long legs, this canid is not a fast runner. It also lacks the stamina needed to chase prey over great distances. Instead, it stalks animals such as rodents by slowly sneaking up on them before making a sudden pounce.

The Jackal-headed God

In ancient Egypt, Anubis, the god of the dead, was shown with a human body and the head of a jackal. This god was believed to be responsible for the process of embalming, which preserved the bodies of the dead. Anubis often appears in wall paintings and sculptures found in burial places. Here he is shown embalming the body of an Egyptian king.

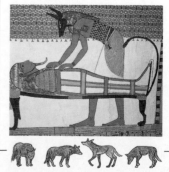

Focus on

The name coyote is from the ancient Aztec word *coyotl*, which means barking dog. These canids are found in most parts of North and Central America, from Costa Rica right up to Alaska and northern Canada. Coyotes eat the same sorts of food as wolves, and the two species are rarely found together. Coyotes are only half the size of wolves, with bodies measuring about 95cm long. They can be recognized by their narrow muzzles, large, pointed ears and long legs. Their tails have a black tip. Coyotes were once thought to be solitary animals, but research has shown that they often live in pairs or small family groups.

COYOTE COUNTRY

A coyote prowls the rocky desert land-scape of Death Valley in California, USA. Coyotes are also known as prairie wolves because they are usually associated with grassy habitat. In fact they inhabit all kinds of different terrain, including mountains, forests, woodlands and desert.

TERRITORIAL MARKING

A coyote marks the boundary of its territory by spraying urine. Coyotes also howl to keep other coyotes off their patch. Like wolves, coyotes use their territory both for hunting and for breeding. Coyote territories, however, are generally much smaller than wolf territories – usually between 14 and 65 sq km in size.

Coyotes

CUNNING HUNTERS

Birds, such as this pheasant, make a tasty meal for coyotes. Coyotes often work in pairs to surround ground-nesting birds or grazing rabbits. They also team up to flush burrowing animals, such as ground squirrels, from their underground homes.

GROWING UP

Two cubs sniff at a freshly killed pheasant brought by their mother. When the cubs are very young, the father brings all the food while the mother stays in the den. Later, she goes out to hunt as well. Most young coyotes leave their parents at the age of one year. A few youngsters stay on to help their parents rear a new litter of cubs.

CLOSE TO HOME

A coyote cub surveys the world from the safety of its den entrance. Dens may be abandoned skunk or badger burrows. Coyotes mate in late winter. Around nine weeks later, the female gives birth to about five cubs. The young feed only on their mother's milk until the age of three weeks, when they start to eat meat as well.

CHICKEN RAID

A coyote peers into a chicken coop, hoping to steal a hen. Coyotes mainly feed on rabbits and rodents. In a way coyotes are actually useful to farmers. They kill large numbers of the unwanted small animals that graze on farmland pasture.

Relatives and Namesakes

Wolves, foxes and other members of the dog family have taken millions of years to evolve (develop). Scientists can trace their history through bones and other fossils preserved in the Earth from ancient times. Somewhere around 65 million years ago, a family of tree-dwelling mammals called miacids developed. These carnivorous mammals tore the flesh from their prey using jagged carnassial teeth similar to those of modern dogs and wolves. Later, around 30 million years ago, one branch of the miacid family evolved into fast-running, mongoose-like creatures called cynodictis. In turn, cynodictis and relatives such as hesperocyon developed into the first distinctively wolf-like creatures. From such ancestors, modern canids evolved around 300,000 years ago.

▲ ANCIENT ANCESTOR

Hesperocyon was the prehistoric ancestor of wolves and other carnivores. It had a long, dog-like snout and sharp carnassial teeth. Over millions of years, hesperocyons had evolved from earlier tree-dwelling creatures, called miacids. Miacids gradually evolved strong legs and feet to make them fast runners.

◄ DIRE WOLVES

The long-extinct dire wolf was an ancient relative of the modern wolf. Remains of these prehistoric creatures have been found in fossil pits in California, USA. Dire wolves lived on Earth about two million years ago. They were fierce predators, much bigger than today's wolves, that preyed on large camelids (camels) and American rhinos (both now extinct) and (the now rare) bison.

◄ WOLF-DOG HYBRID

A wolf-dog skirts farmland in Italy. This animal is the offspring of a grey wolf and a German shepherd dog. Coy-wolves, red wolves and coy-dogs are other hybrids that resulted from interbreeding between coyotes, wolves and domestic dogs. These animals may resemble domestic dogs, but they cannot usually be tamed.

Tasmanian wolf
(Thylacinus cynocephalus)

TASMANIAN WOLVES ►

This engraving of the 1800s shows two thylacines, or Tasmanian wolves. As the name suggests, these creatures lived on the island of Tasmania, off Australia. With their long snouts and strong legs, thylacines looked a lot like wild dogs and barked like dogs, too. However, they were marsupials, a group of mammals that carries its young in pouches. Their natural prey was kangaroos and wallabies, but when they started to take sheep farmers hunted them to extinction.

Did you know? Dogs have been domesticated for at least 15,000 years.

▲ SCAVENGERS AT WORK

Hyenas gather at a Kenyan waterhole to finish off a buffalo killed by lions. Hyenas look like African hunting dogs, but are from the *Hyaenidae* family. They can crunch through the toughest bones with their powerful jaws and strong, sharp teeth.

▲ DESCENDED FROM ONE ANCESTOR

All domestic dogs are descended from the wolf. Human and dog came together thousands of years ago for mutual benefit. By Roman times, around 500BC, many of the breeds we know today had already developed.

Focus on

BIG EARS

The fennec is the world's smallest fox, but it has the biggest ears. Fennec foxes live in the sandy deserts of Africa and Arabia. Their very large ears help to give off heat and keep the animals cool in the scorching desert. The fox rests in its cool, sandy burrow by day, and comes out to hunt rodents, lizards and insects at night.

With their large, pointed ears and long snouts, foxes look a lot like coyotes, but have shorter legs. There are more than 20 species of fox. They are found in most places, but are not native to Australia, South-east Asia or Antarctica. Like other canids, foxes are very adaptable and live in a wide variety of habitats, from the frozen Arctic and bare mountainsides to scorching deserts and crowded cities. Foxes eat almost anything, including small mammals, birds, reptiles, insects, worms and fruit. Most are solitary hunters that keep other foxes away from their territories. In the breeding season, they yelp harshly to find a mate. Litters of up to six cubs are born in a burrow or rocky crevice.

Arctic fox in winter coat *(Alopex lagopus)*

Arctic fox in summer coat *(Alopex lagopus)*

SNOWY WANDERER

Arctic foxes roam over the freezing, wind-swept Arctic tundra. They feed on lemmings (rodents) and sometimes follow polar bears to steal the leftovers from their kills.

BRAND NEW COAT

In spring, the Arctic fox's thick white fur falls out. A new dark brown coat grows in its place. This blends in well with the rocks and plants of the tundra after the snow has melted.

Foxes

Crab-eating fox
(Cerdocyon thous)

NIGHT RAIDER

Red foxes live in woods and open country in North America, Europe and Asia, and were introduced into Australia after 1780. They kill their prey by springing upwards and then pouncing, to trap their victims in their front paws. Red foxes have moved into towns, where they find food by raiding rubbish bins at night.

CRAB-EATING FOX

The crab-eating fox lives in the grasslands, woods and swamps of South America. As well as crabs, these foxes hunt a wide range of other animals, including lizards, frogs, rodents and chickens. They also steal reptiles' eggs. The species earned its rather misleading name because the first animal to be spotted by a scientist had a crab in its mouth.

COLPEO

A pair of colpeo foxes rest by a rocky outcrop in the Andes Mountains of Bolivia. This South American fox lives mainly on grasslands and in mountains. Its tawny-black fur provides camouflage among the boulders, where it hunts for mice, birds, eggs and snakes.

Colpeo fox
(Dusicyon culpaeus)

▲ TALL TALE
In 1901, a pack of wolves was reported to have attacked and eaten a group of five Romanian soldiers. Suspiciously, no trace of the men was left except their blood-stained weapons. This event is hard to believe, since even starving wolves would be unlikely to attack a band of well-armed men.

Fact or Fiction?

Myths, fairytales and even modern films depict wolves as bold, wicked hunters that prey on humans, especially young children. In fact, there have been very few confirmed accounts of wolves attacking people, and none in North America, one of the animal's main strongholds. Wolves were more likely to have been a menace in Europe before guns were invented. Then, they probably had little fear of humans and may have prowled close to villages in the hope of stealing sheep and other domestic beasts. Wolves may have acquired their reputation as man-eaters by scavenging meat from dead bodies on battlefields. In modern times, the rare attacks on people have probably been made by wolves suffering from rabies, a disease that drives animals mad.

◄ ALWAYS ALERT
A modern-day shepherd tends his flock in the remote Spanish mountains. He has only his dogs and a stout stick to scare away any wolves that threaten his flock. An experienced shepherd, however, knows that wolves are easily frightened.

▲ WOLF MAGIC

Native Americans thought of wolves as magical creatures. This shaman (medicine man) is dressed in a wolf skin to take on the creature's power. He calls upon the wolf spirit to give his patient the strength to recover from illness.

▲ HOWLING AT THE MOON

Werewolves are a popular subject of horror films. In folk tales, these are humans who turn into wolves when there is a full moon. They can only be killed by a silver bullet.

▲ WOLVES BLAMED FOR ATTACK

In 1907, wolves were said to have attacked a group of Hungarian gypsies. There was no real proof, however, and the attack may have been carried out by a gang of robbers.

◀ SLY OLD FOX

In this scene from one of *Aesop's Fables*, a clever vixen (female fox) tries to outwit a cockerel crowing at dawn. She says to the cockerel that she would like to embrace the owner of such a fine voice. Wolves and foxes are portrayed as villains in many folk tales and legends. They are frequently described as sly and cunning, terms that show them in a negative light.

Natural Enemies

Wolves and wild dogs may be powerful predators, but they face many threats in the wild. Their natural enemies include the largest creatures that they hunt, such as moose, bison and musk oxen. Their sharp hooves and horns can fatally wound a predator. One careless slip, and a wolf may be gored or trampled to death. Wolves and wild dogs are also threatened when their habitats are disturbed or destroyed. In many areas, the territories where wild dogs can roam free are getting smaller and smaller. Land is needed for crops or to graze herds of sheep and cattle. Forests are cut down for timber or to make way for new roads and towns. The survival of wolves and wild dogs is also threatened by deadly diseases such as distemper, anthrax and rabies.

▲ HUNTING THE HUNTERS
A lioness has killed an African hunting dog. Groups of lions are known to stalk and ambush hunting dogs while they feed on a kill, or drink at waterholes. Hyenas and jackals also prey on hunting dogs. They sneak up to the den and steal young pups if the adult dogs are not keeping a careful watch.

▼ DEFENCE TACTICS
On the Arctic tundra, large, shaggy musk oxen form a defensive ring around their young. Their long, fierce horns face outwards, keeping young and weak members of the herd safe from wolves.

◄ DANGEROUS TARGET

A moose browses among the tall lakeside shrubs in Wyoming, USA. Moose are powerful beasts. An adult male stands 2m tall at the shoulder and weighs as much as ten wolves. Its antlers and hooves can inflict great damage. A moose can crack a wolf's skull with one mighty kick, or gore it with its antlers and toss it high in the air. Wolves must be very wary when hunting such dangerous prey.

DINGOES KEEP OUT ►

A dingo attacks a sheep, snapping at its hindquarters. Farmers have built a great fence across 5,300km of south-eastern Australia to keep dingoes out of sheep country. Any dog caught inside the fence is shot.

▲ DEADLY RABIES

A black-backed jackal lies dying of rabies. Rabies is a fatal disease that attacks the brain and nervous system. It is passed on by saliva from an infected bite. Wild dogs have been wiped out in many areas to prevent rabies spreading to humans, even though a vaccine is available.

▲ KEEP OFF THE ROAD

African hunting dogs roam along a newly built road that cuts across their territory in the bush. They are scavenging for road-kills, but may well become victims themselves. The rapid human development of the dogs' territory threatens their way of life and very survival.

57

Wolves and People

Wherever wolves and wild dogs come into contact with people, the animals are regarded as dangerous pests who will – given the chance – kill livestock. They are poisoned, trapped and shot, not only for their skins, but for sport. Wolves were once the most widespread carnivores in the northern hemisphere. Now they survive in a much reduced area, often in small, scattered groups. Several species are endangered, including the Simien wolf, the red wolf and the African hunting dog. Much of the land where these animals once lived is now being farmed. Dholes and bush dogs have also become very rare as their forest habitat is destroyed. Some species, such as the Falkland Island wolf, a kind of fox, are already extinct.

NORTH AMERICA

SOUTH AMERICA

grey wolf territories

▲ WOLF HUNT
In the Middle Ages domestic dogs were often used to kill wolves, as this Dutch engraving of 1880 shows. The last wolves were wiped out in England by 1500 and in Ireland by 1800.

Tame Wolf
This book is a first edition of the popular novel White Fang *by American writer Jack London. Set in northern Canada, it describes how a wolf, named White Fang, is tamed and becomes a pet. In general it is not against the law to keep a wolf as a pet, but countries with restrictions require owners to have a special permit. The* Call of the Wild *by the same author describes how a pet dog joins a wolf pack and becomes wild.*

WHITE FANG

JACK LONDON

◀ NOWHERE TO RUN

A hunter in Colorado, USA, shoulders a coyote he has shot. In country areas, farmers shoot or poison coyotes because they steal sheep and other livestock and spread disease. Elsewhere, when coyotes and other wild dogs enter towns to scrounge scraps, they risk being shot as pests.

▲ WOLF TERRITORY

Grey wolves once had the greatest range of any wild land mammal. In the past, wolves were once common right across North America, throughout Europe, the Middle East and most of Asia. Their present range shows they have been exterminated in most of Mexico and the USA, in almost all of western Europe and over much of Asia.

▼ AN UNKIND LUXURY

Fox fur was very fashionable in the early 1900s, mainly for coats and for trimming garments. The fox fur stole (scarf) shown here uses the pelt (fur and skin) of an entire animal. In the past, furs were worn mainly to keep warm in winter. Today, however, man-made fabrics are as warm as fur, making it unnecessary and cruel to kill these animals for their pelts.

▲ UNDER THREAT

A Simien wolf howls high in the Ethiopian mountains. As the human population grows, more land is farmed and the animal's range is restricted. Simien wolves are shot for fur and killed by farmers as pests. There may be only 500 Simien wolves left in the wild.

Conservation

In many parts of the world, efforts are being made to save threatened wolves and wild dogs. Grey wolves have recently been reintroduced into areas where they had died out. Conservationists working to protect wolves face opposition from local farmers who fear that wolves will kill their livestock. In some reserves, wolves and wild dogs have begun to be promoted as tourist attractions. This helps people to learn about these animals and the entrance fees help to finance conservation work. Today, wolves and their relatives are gradually losing their bad image. More and more people are appreciating their admirable qualities – intelligence, loyalty and strong family ties. In the wild, these predators actually help to improve stocks of prey animals. By hunting mostly weak or sickly individuals, they help to ensure the survival of the fittest.

▲ SUCCESS STORY
Conservationists release a red wolf that was bred in captivity into a reserve in North Carolina, USA. Red wolves were once found throughout the south-eastern states. They almost became extinct, but breeding programmes have saved the species.

◄ RADIO TRACKING
A red wolf has been fitted with a radio collar. The collar allows scientists to track the animal as it roams the wilds. Radio tracking helps to provide scientists with valuable information about the wolf's habits and range. Increasing such knowledge also helps conservationists with their work.

▲ STAR OF THE SHOW

Tourists on safari photograph African hunting dogs in a reserve. In recent years, such tourist attractions have earned much-needed cash for remote villages. The money helps to persuade local people not to hunt the dogs, but to see them as a valuable asset instead.

▲ HELPING TO KEEP THE BALANCE

A pack of wolves feeds on a deer carcass. By targeting old and sick animals, the wolves actually help the rest of the herd to survive. They may be removing a deer whose sickness could infect others in the herd, or an old animal whose share of food could be better used to rear healthy young.

▼ SOUND OF THE WILD

For many people, the wolf is a symbol of the wilderness. Now in some countries, wolves are becoming a tourist attraction. At some centres, members of the public can even walk alongside tame wolves, petting them if they wish, accompanied, of course, by expert handlers.

▲ WOLF RESEARCH

Scientists check the teeth of a drugged Arctic wolf. Researchers sometimes capture the same wolves several times over the course of a number of years to study their life histories. This work helps to provide evidence of the strong family ties and keen intelligence of the wolf.

61

GLOSSARY

carnassials
The jagged teeth towards the back of a wolf's mouth, that are used for cutting up meat.

carnivore
An animal that feeds mainly on the flesh of other animals.

adapt
When an animal or group of animals changes – physically or in behaviour – in order to survive in new conditions.

carrion
The body of a dead animal.

conservationist
A person who works to protect the Earth's natural resources, including animals and plants.

alpha pair
The top male and female in a wolf pack. Only this strong, healthy pair of animals breeds.

cub
A young wolf or dog.

binocular vision
The ability to see things with both eyes at the same time, which helps animals to judge distances well and pounce on prey.

den
The home of an animal such as a wolf or fox. A den may be an underground burrow or a cave, or simply a nest in the long grass.

camouflage
The colours and patterns on an animal's body that help it to blend in with its surroundings so it can hide from enemies or sneak up on prey.

canid
A member of the dog family. Wolves, jackals, coyotes and foxes are all canids.

dew claw
The toe found high on a wolf's foreleg, which does not touch the ground. It has no obvious use, so it is probably used for grooming.

diet
The range of food an animal eats.

canines
The sharp, pointed teeth near the front of a wolf's jaw, which are used for seizing and killing prey.

domesticated
Describes animals that have been tamed by people. Cows, sheep and horses are all domesticated.

Equator
An imaginary line running around the centre of the Earth, separating north from south.

evolve
When a species of animals or plants changes gradually over time, to become better suited to the conditions in which it lives.

extinct
When a whole species of animals has died out completely, so that none is left.

fossil
The remains of plants or animals that have turned to stone over thousands or millions of years.

gland
An organ of the body that makes chemicals for a particular use.

habitat
A type of place where certain animals and plants live, such as a tropical rainforest or a desert.

hierarchy
A strict social order within a group of animals.

hybrid
The offspring of two animals from different species or subspecies.

litter
A group of young animals born to a mother at one time.

mammal
A warm-blooded animal with a bony skeleton and hair on its body. Female mammals produce milk from mammary glands (equivalent to human breasts) to feed their young.

moult
To shed fur or feathers.

muzzle
The jaws and nose of an animal such as a wolf.

nocturnal
Describes an animal that rests by day and is active during the hours of darkness.

pack
The name given to a group of wolves or wild dogs that lives and hunts together.

predator
An animal that hunts other creatures for food.

prey
An animal that is hunted by another animal for food.

range
The area in which an animal species lives.

regurgitate
When an animal brings up half-digested food to feed its young.

rendezvous
A meeting place that lies in the heart of a wolf pack's territory. This is a safe place where wolves gather and cubs play.

rodent
An animal with chisel-shaped front teeth used for gnawing.

savanna
Open grassland found in warm, wet tropical regions around the Equator.

scavenger
An animal that feeds on rubbish, dead animals and the remains of carcasses left behind by other predators.

social
Describes animals that live together in large family groups.

stalk
When a hunting animal follows its prey cautiously to avoid being seen until close enough to pounce.

submissive
When a junior animal gives way to a more powerful animal.

territory
An area that an animal uses for feeding or breeding, and defends against others of its species.

tundra
The cold, treeless lowlands of the far north. Summers are very short here. During the winter the sun hardly rises in the sky and it is dark for most of the day.

wean
When a young animal moves from drinking only its mother's milk to a diet of solid food.

INDEX